Letterheads and Stamps of the Interwar Japanese Diplomatic Missions in the Baltic States

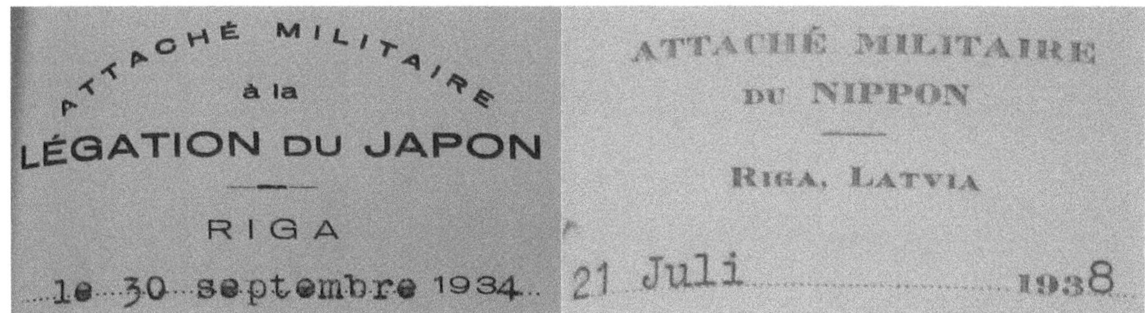

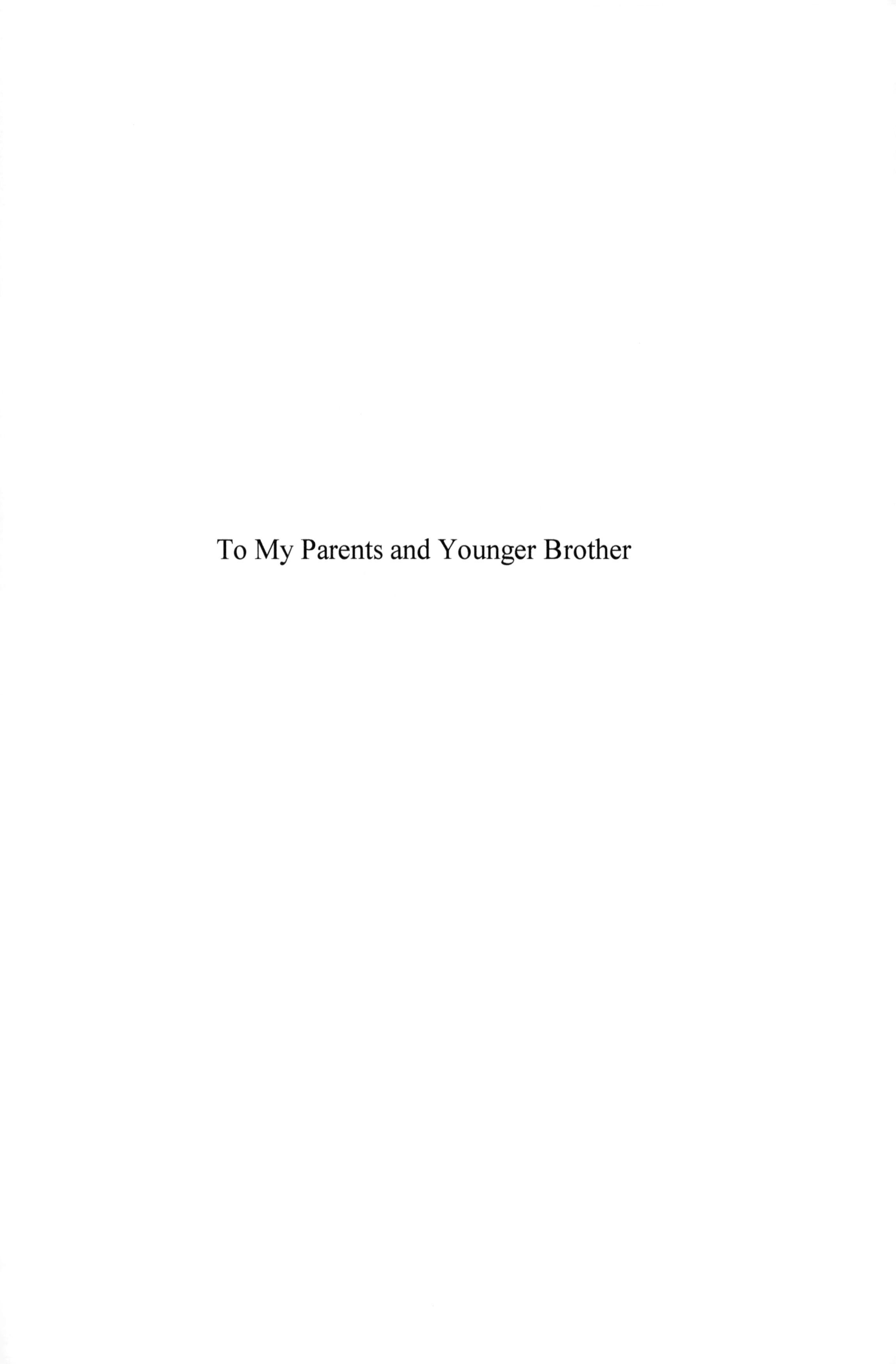

To My Parents and Younger Brother

The Inter-War Japanese Military Intelligence Activities in the Baltic States: 1919-1940

Shingo Masunaga

Doctoral Candidate
University of Turku

Author Note

Shingo Masunaga, Centre for East Asian Studies (CEAS), Department of Philosophy, University of Turku. Shingo Masunaga is currently a Doctoral candidate of the Centre for East Asian Studies. Correspondence concerning this book should be addressed to him.

E-mails: shingo.masunaga@utu.fi (Primary)

shingomasunaga7@gmail.com

ISBN 978-1-387-00565-9

First Edition

Shingo Masunaga 増永 真悟

• Date of Birth: February 20th 1988 (29 years old)

• Nationality: JAPAN

Degrees:

Master (MA) in Social Sciences,

Tallinn University (2015)

Bachelor (BA) in International Communication,

Kansai Gaidai University (2010)

Publications:

1. **Masunaga, S. (2017).** ***Sarkans Junijs: Military Relationship between the Baltic States and Japan.*** **Nagoya, Japan: International Academic Forum (IAFOR). Page 45-49.**
http://iafor.org/archives/proceedings/APSec/APSec2016_proceedings.pdf

2. **Masunaga, S. (2016)** ***Emerging Japanese Nationalism and Its Correlations with the Collapse of Japan as a Family Nation.*** **Northridge, CA, the United States: California State University Northridge.**
http://scholarworks.csun.edu/handle/10211.3/174801

3. **Masunaga, S. (February 9, 2015)** ***Is an Asian NATO on the Horizon?*** **Prague, Czech Republic: NATO Information Centre Prague.**
http://data.idnes.cz/soubory/na_zpravy/A150217_M02_022_150209_MASUNAGA.PDF

Introduction

Recently, researchers have shown an increased interest on the Interwar Japanese military intelligence activities. The book 'In the shore of the Baltic Sea' (*Baruto-kai no Horoti Nite*) published in 1985, by Yuriko Onodera, wife of Japanese military attaché Makoto Onodera in Riga residence (1936-38), has been a must-read book for those who are interested in Japanese military intelligence activities in the Baltic Sea region. Still, until recent years, the details of the Japanese military intelligence activities in the Baltic States were never unveiled, mainly due to the restrictions on the access to the classified documents. After six decades since the end of the WW2, a portion of the records was finally released in both the Baltic States and the Western countries which carefully observed Japan's diplomatic actions back then.

In 2012, Noboru Okabe published the award-winning non-fiction book 'Disappeared Yalta report: The struggle of intelligence officer Makoto Onodera' (*Kieta Yalta Mitsuyaku Kinkyuden: Jyoho-Shikan Onodera Makoto no Kodokuna Tatakai*), based on the declassified materials acquired from the British and the U.S. national archives such as the intercepted correspondence between Japanese army offices in Europe and Tokyo. Moreover, he was able to access Onodera's unreleased personal memoir through his family. Yet, his focus was on Onodera's 'wartime' intelligence activities in Stockholm (1941-45). His previous life in Riga (1936-38) was briefly described in some pages, but with notable mistakes especially on some facts and person's names.

The documents Okabe mainly referred were the so-called 'Onodera reports' issued in 1946 by the Strategic Services Unit (SSU), counter-intelligence branch of the famous OSS (Office of Strategic Services), based on the interrogations of ex-Japanese army officers including Onodera and Onouchi, the last military attaché in Riga (1939-40), at the Sugamo prison in Tokyo. It was declassified in 2005 and now is opened to public at the Central Information Agency (CIA)'s official website. Presumably, they are the only sources available today regarding the details of the Interwar Japanese military intelligence activities in the Baltic States. Meanwhile, Okabe (2012) found both Onodera and Onouchi made some 'false' statements against the SSU interrogation officers in order to protect the identities of the ex-informants and collaborators worked for them. Thus, the over-reliance on the U.S. reports would result in a tragedy of unwillingly constructed 'Conspiracy theory'.

On the other hand, some decades later, just before the passing in 1987, Onodera himself left some memoirs which were never officially published, but preserved at Japanese governmental and private archives. It is a precious information source alongside the U.S. reports as none of the other Japanese military attachés to Latvia left anything like that and majority of the official documents were burnt down or lost amidst the confusion of the Soviet occupation of the Baltic States in 1940 and the defeat of Japan in 1945. With regard to the reliability of the 'unpublished' memoirs, Setsuko, the second daughter of Onodera, said that the memoir of her mother Yuriko was totally based on the father's memoirs. Thus, from the principle of cross-checking, I found it reliable.

Additionally, I acquired the documents regarding the Riga army office from Estonian, Latvian, and Japanese archives. The best remaining sources in Japan were the official documents survived the war and preserved at the National Institute for Defence Studies (NIDS) Archive in Tokyo whereas those in the Baltic States were actually articles on periodicals (newspapers, the Armies's official magazines such as *Sõdur* of Estonia and *Latvijas Kareivis* of Latvia) available at the national libraries. Combining the primary and secondary sources from the four countries (Latvia, Estonia, Japan, and the U.S.), it finally became possible to gain perspective on the Riga army office.

The findings suggest that the Riga army office was involved not only in the ordinary military information gathering, but also the joint Estonian-Japanese intelligence operation to politically topple the Soviet Union by using the émigré activists. Although I could not find out the evidences to prove the existence of such ambitious operation, most of Estonian war history professionals whom I contacted by e-mail such as Professor Ivo Juurvee of Estonian national police academy (*Sisekaitseakadeemia*) and Mr. Toe Nõmm of the Estonian Ministry of

Defence clearly denied it from one reason: Too risky to be unveiled. They said, in the small society of the Interwar Estonia, it was difficult to conceal such big deal from the eyes of public and the censorship on media under the Konstantin Päts administration, often considered as a development dictatorship, was not strongly enforced.

Indeed, the details of the operation were only mentioned in the U.S. reports and Onodera's unpublished memoirs. Even a single word regarding the operation did not appear in the memoirs of Estonian intelligence officers (Villem Saarsen and Richard Maasing) who fled to Sweden after the Soviet occupation of their homeland. Ofcourse, there is a possibility that Russian archives (especially the Central Military Archive in Moscow) hold some documents about the operation, but due to my poor Russian language skill and the lack of knowledge on conducting fieldwork in Russia, no Russian sources were used in this article. What we can assume by the existing evidences is that the operation was maybe much smaller in its scale and less influential than what had previously been confessed by Onodera.

1. Roles of Japanese Military Attachés and Definition of 'Espionage'

In the Interwar period, between 1919 and 1940, the Imperial Japanese Army (hereafter 'Japanese Army') had ordered 'special missions' to their offices in Northern Europe. These orders were supervised by first, the Army office in Warsaw[1], and then from circa 1937, the Army office in Berlin.[2] The main reason for the choice of the Warsaw Army office was that the mature relationship between Japanese and Polish military forces ever since the latter nation's independence.

According to Bowyer (2007), 'Espionage' is "the use of spies, surveillance equipment, etc., in order to collect information about the enemy." (p.87-88). To be precise, in the realm of military affairs, it can be categorized into several

[1] The Warsaw Army office was located inside the Japanese Legation in Poland (Address: Foksal 10 – the street later renamed 'Pileckiego').

[2] The Berlin Army office (Address: Nollendorf strasse 2) was independent from the Japanese Legation in Germany. The Nollendorf building was spontaneously acquired by Colonel Hiroshi Oshima (1934-1939)

sections. Among them, HUMINT (Human Intelligence) and OSINT (Open Source Intelligence) were the two pillars of the Interwar Japanese military intelligence activities in Europe. The former involves the collection of information through informants, including spies, and the latter is a compilation of analyses on information opened to the public e.g. newspaper articles.

However, objectives given to Japanese military attachés in Central and Northern Europe were far beyond this narrow definition of 'Espionage'. It included attempts to topple foreign regimes and HUMINT (Human Intelligence) also known as 'spying' by penetrated agents on foreign soils.

2. Inauguration of the Baltic-Japanese Diplomatic Relations

The Baltic States (Estonia, Latvia, and Lithuania) has long been suffered in a 'crack' of the power struggles of the great powers. Starting from German invasions circa 1200, the region has been either a buffer zone, in peacetime, or a battlefield at the great power's hegemonic wars.

The first Japanese who focused on the Baltic geopolitical circumstance was Colonel Motojiro Akashi, Japanese intelligence officer during the Russo-Japanese War who succeeded the secret operation to organize anti-Tsar movements by mobilizing activists inside the Russian Empire such as Konni Zilliacus of Finland and Evno Azef of Russia. Based in Japanese Legation to Sweden in Stockholm, Akashi hired a young diplomat called Sentaro Ueda, who studied at Petersburg University in St. Petersburg before the war and fluent in Russian language, as his personal secretary. The activities of Akashi involved number of ethnic minorities not only Finns and Russians, but also Estonians and Latvians. Alongside Japanese victory on the war, it was probably the first point of contact between the Baltic races and Japanese. Anyway, it took another decade to establish vis-à-vis relations, only after the former gained the first-ever independences after WW1.

The inauguration of Estonian-Japanese diplomatic relations dates back to 1919. Ants Piip, member of the Estonian Foreign Mission in London who became

Foreign Minister in 1930s, made a courtesy call to the Ambassador Sutemi Chinda of Japan to the United Kingdom and delivered a formal message from the Estonian government to request Japanese recognition of the state. (Tokyo Asahi Shimbun, March 23rd 1919, p.2). Upon this request from the newly independent Baltic Republic, Tokyo made a 'provisional recognition' of Estonia following the decisions of the United Kingdom, France, and Italy. The decision of the Japanese government was notified to Piip by Chinda on March 15th. Later in the same year, Latvia was also given the recognition by Japan, but unlike Estonia, it was a formal recognition of the state. (Tokyo Asahi Shimbun, March 13th 1920, p.3) Lithuania had to wait until December 1922 for formal Japanese recognition due to the Polish-Lithuanian War (1919-1920) and the Klaipeda (Memel) territorial dispute with Poland in the aftermath of the War. (Tokyo Asahi Shimbun, December 24th 1922, p.1) By 1923, all the Baltic States were granted formal recognition by Japan.

In 1921, diplomat Seigo Sasaki of Japanese Legation in Stockholm sent to establish a diplomat office in Reval (Tallinn). (Päewaleht, 1921, p.4) Tokyo was eager to know the transition of political situations in the Soviet Union as all the Japanese diplomatic missions in the country were forced to close down by the end of 1910s and Reval, a capital of newly independent Estonian republic, appeared to be the best spot for the observation. That was the special mission given to Sasaki. Approved by the MoFA, Sasaki hired at least one local Russian informant who was specialized in espionage, at annual rate of 1,500 Yen. (JACAR, B03040748900) Two years later, in May 1923, First Secretary Sentaro Ueda of the Warsaw Legation, along with Secretary Kozo Izumi, was sent to Riga to establish a new diplomat office. (JACAR, Ref.B15100944400) Ueda was a far well-experienced diplomat compared to Sasaki in terms of Russian affairs.

Also, compared to Reval (Tallinn), Riga was a far bigger city and it was more convenient in terms of hiring the informants and the collection of open source information.

Figure 1. The apartment of *Andreja Pumpura iela* 6, Riga. (February 2017)
The Riga diplomat office was located in this building.

At the same time, considering the geopolitical importance of Latvia in the intelligence activities against the Soviet Union emphasized by the First Secretary Ueda, the MoA also decided to send army officers to Latvia in the name of 'researchers on the Soviet affairs'. Consequently, the Reval diplomatic office was closed in 1922 and the mission was succeeded by Ueda. In March 1924, Assistant military attaché of the Berlin Embassy visited Riga with Captain Noritsune Shimizu, the army's researcher resided in Germany. At that time, Japanese military attaché to the Soviet Union was declared '*persona non grata*' due to Japan's Siberian intervention (1918-1922) and instead sent to Germany. But, he planned to move its office to Latvia because of its geopolitical advantage in intelligence against the Soviet Union. Therefore, after the return of the assistant attaché, Shimizu was ordered to remain in Riga, expected to be a liaison officer between the assistant attaché and Ueda. However, the plan faced Ueda's complete denial from the perspective of diplomatic protocols[3] thus had

[3] Ueda told Shimizu that 'Military Attaché' is a position requires to be formally accredited by the local

to be abandoned.(JACAR, Ref.B15100944400)

After Shimizu, in January 1926, Major Torashiro Kawabe[4] was assigned to the second researcher in Riga residence. (JACAR, Ref. C01006107900). Except the case of Shimizu, main task of the Riga-based researchers was to master Russian language and also collect information about the Soviet military affairs as much as possible. Kawabe arrived in Riga on March 1st via Moscow.(Kawabe, 1962, p.46) The diplomatic relation between Japan and the Soviet Union was restored a year ago (The Soviet–Japanese Basic Convention on February 26th 1925) hence it was possible for him to travel by the Siberian railway. Along with Captain Genzo Yanagida[5], who arrived to Riga in early 1927 (JACAR, Ref. C01006039400), the only two Japanese citizens in Latvia concentrated on improving Russian language skills and sometimes travelled around Europe.

After returning to Tokyo in 1928, Kawabe submitted the report on 'Special military facilities based on the landscape of the Soviet Union' (JACAR, Ref.C01003722800) However, in his memoir published in 1960s, Kawabe described "there was no way to conduct such thing (the research on the Soviet military affairs) in Riga, but just saw the drastic improvement in Russian language skill". (Kawabe, 1962, p.52).

---

government based on the existence of the previously accredited diplomat (Envoy or Ambassador). Thus, in order to implement the Army's plan, it required the MoFA to send, at least, a chargé d'affaires to Riga and officially promote the current diplomat office to 'Legation'.(JACAR, Ref.B11500944400) The latter ministry did not have a budget to spare with the plan due to the austere fiscal policy ever since the Great Kanto Earthquake in September 1923.

[4] In late 1930s, Kawabe became a military attaché to Germany (1938-39). At the end of the WW2, he was Vice Chief of Staff of the General Staff at the rank of Lieutenant General. According to some sources, he established 'Kawabe Organ' in 1948, in which the objective was Japan's rearmament. Passed in 1960. Aged 69.

[5] He was later appointed as military attaché to Poland and Romania (1932-1934), chief of the secret military agency in Harbin (1940), and commander of Port Arthur fortress in China at the end of the WW2. Arrested by the Soviet forces in August 1945 and passed in Moscow, 1952 during the internment. Aged 59.

Figure 2. Captain Genzo Yanagida (first from the left, front row) at the 10th Independence Day parade in Riga, Latvia. (November 18th 1928) There was also Captain Kitsujyu Ayabe[6] (first from the right), the Army's researcher in the Soviet Union.
Courtesy: Estonian Film Archive (*Eesti filmiarhiiv*)

In 1928, while Captain Yanagida was still in Riga, Japan and Latvia mutually ratified the Treaty of Commerce and Navigation, the first-ever bilateral diplomatic agreement between Japan and any of the Baltic States. Under such circumstance, the Japanese Ministry of Foreign Affairs (MoFA) planned to establish the first diplomatic mission in Latvia. (Tokyo Asahi Shimbun, July 5th 1928, p.1) On 1st October 1929, the Legation of Japan in Latvia was finally established. (Tokyo Asahi Shimbun, September 4th 1929, p.3) Ambassador Harukazu Nagaoka to Germany also hold the position of the first Envoy to Latvia and Infantry Colonel Shigeyasu Suzuki[7] of the Warsaw Legation was accredited as the first, but non-resident, military attaché to Latvia. He participated in the ceremony of presentation of credentials to Latvian President Gustavs Zemgals

---

[6] Captain Ayabe was the Army's researcher in Moscow residence (1928-1930). As of December 1941, he was Deputy Chief of Staff of the Kwantung Army. He saw the end of the WW2 as Chief of Staff of the Seventh Area Army in Singapore. Passed on February 14th 1980.

[7] Colonel Suzuki was incorporated into the reserve duty in December 1938, at the rank of Lieutenant General. During the WW2, he served as Chairman of the Automobile Control Association. Passed on June 1st 1957.

with Captain Seiichi Terada[8] and Captain Minoru Sasaki[9], his subordinates in Warsaw. (Latvijas Kareivis, October 30th 1928, p.1)

Figure 3. Japanese military officers in Tartu, Estonia. (July 29th 1929)
Colonel Shigeyasu Suzuki (first from the left, person with aiguillette), Captain Kitsujyu Ayabe (sitting in the centre), Captain Minoru Sasaki (third from the left), and Captain Seiichi Terada (second from the right, sitting next to Estonian officer) were confirmed.
Courtesy: Estonian National Archive (*Eesti rahvusarhiiv*)

3. Thoughts on the Baltic-Japanese Military Relations

In the Interwar period, Latvia and the rest of the Baltic States were often called '*Cordon Sanitaire*' (Sanitary Cordon), the political wall to reject the infiltration of the Soviet Communism into (Western) Europe, first claimed by Georges Clemenceau in March 1919. After the revolution, Japan immediately defined the Soviet Communism as a threat to the 'national polity' (*Kokutai*) which based on the reign of the Emperor, and enforced the Maintenance of the Public Order Act

[8] Captain Terada was the Army's researcher in Warsaw residence (1927-1929).He became the first Japanese military attaché to Finland (1934-1936) by the recommendation of Lieutenant Colonel Tsutomu Ouchi, then military attaché to Latvia (1933-1935). At the end of the WW2, Terada was Deputy Chief of Staff of the Air General Army at the rank of Lieutenant General. Passed on March 8th 1969.

[9] Captain Sasaki was also the Army's researcher in Warsaw residence (1927-1929). During the WW2, he commanded the army units of New Georgia in 1943 and saw the end of the war in Rabaul Island, at the rank of Lieutenant General. Passed on April 27th 1961.

(Chian-Iji Hou) in 1925 to regulate the domestic Communist movements. For both Baltic States and Japan, the Soviet Communism was an imminent threat and its 'containment' became a common political goal.

In fact, Japan had previously intervened Russian Civil War following the Communist Revolution in 1917 by supporting the army of ex-Admiral Alexander Kolchak, one of the dissident groups (White Army) against the Communists, and occupying West Siberia by their own military forces alongside other great powers e.g. France and the United States. While the attempts of the existing great powers to clash the world's first Communist regime were proceeding, ex-Russian territories on the other side of the globe such as Estonian and Latvia were fighting their own wars for independence. In February 1920, Kolchak was executed by the red army. By the end of the year, the defeat of the white army became clear and Japan suffered from battered economy due to the decrease in exports after the end of the WW1 and on the other hand, the increase of military expenditures on the prolonged interventions to the Soviet Union.

During this period, from late 1910s to 1920s, Captain Michitaro Komatsubara[10], was detached to Estonia from the Army General Staff in Tokyo and resided in Tallinn between 1919 and 1922. His mission was to report the political situations of the Soviet Union and the Baltic States to Tokyo. Given the status of 'military representative of Japanese Army' (*Jaapani sõjaväe esindaja*) by the Estonian government, Komatsubara was provided an access to the classified information e.g. moves of the Estonian Army and had a close relationship with General Johan Laidoner, Commander of the Estonian 1st Division. Likewise, Lieutenant Colonel Kenichi Ikenaka[11] of Japanese Navy was stationed in Riga from 1924 to 1925.

---

[10] Komatsubara later became a military attaché to the Soviet Union (1927-30). According to Kuromiya (2011), the Soviet counterintelligence honey trapped him in Moscow and used him an agent inside Japanese Army throughout 1930s. In 1938, he was appointed as the commander of the 23rd division stationed in Hailaer. The division was almost annihilated in the battle of Khalkhin Gol (Nomonhan) with the Soviet Union in Summer 1939. Passed from stomach cancer on October 6th 1940. Aged 54.

[11] Ikenaka's residence in Riga was Ausekla iela 7. After the task in Latvia, he was promoted to a naval military attaché to the Soviet Union (June-October 1925).Passed on August 21st 1954.

Figure 4. Captain Michitaro Komatsubara, inspects the Estonian 4th infantry regiment in Narva front. (Summer 1919)
Courtesy: Estonian Film Archive (*Eesti filmiarhiiv*)

The Baltic impressions of Japanese were good. It was largely due to the experiences of the Baltic volunteers during the Russo-Japanese War (1904-05) such as Aleksander Tõnisson, who became Estonian defence minister in early 1930s, and Captain Bock, German Latvian who served as an adjutant of General Yevgeni Alekseyev, Viceroy of the Russian Far East. Also, the book 'Russo-Japanese War' written by former Russian War Minister Viktor Sakharov was translated into the three languages of the Baltic States. Although it was written by the ex-enemy political giant, Japanese were praised as *'Surprising well-educated and disciplined people'* (the excerpt from the introduction of the Estonian version). But, the biggest influence of the Russo-Japanese War on the Baltic populace was Japanese victory over the Russian Baltic fleet in Tsushima. Estonian and Latvian newspapers reported the result of this historic battle on time (by translating the reports on British and French newspapers), which was very surprising fact under the Imperial Russian rule, and the people soon knew the 'symbol of the Russian military might', if not oppression, over the Baltic Sea region was completely vanished in the sea of the Far East.

In case of Estonians, we could also add the 'ethnic background' as the root of their close tie with Japanese. Makoto Onodera, Japanese military attaché in Riga from 1936 to 1938, stated "As being Asian race (Finns), Estonians had a great sympathy with Japan and Japanese from the same reason of Finland. I found Estonia as a 'treasure house' of information. This was one of the great successes (during my duty in Riga)". (Okabe, 2014, p.83).

4. History of the Japanese Army Office in Riga (1931-1940)

In August 1933, Lieutenant Colonel Tsutomu Ouchi, the second Japanese military attaché in Riga residence, established the army office in the apartment of *Elizabetes iela* (Elizabeth Street) 33 upon his arrival. According to Makoto Onodera, the third Japanese military attaché in Riga residence (1936-1938), the Elizabetes office was inconvenient due to 'lack of spaces'. In May 1937, the Riga army office found a new residence in *Baznīcas iela* (Church Street) 19. It was only a block away from Estonian Legation in Riga (*Skolas iela* 13) where Lieutenant Colonel Villem Saarsen, one of Onodera's best friends and collaborator in the joint intelligence operations against the Soviet Union, worked.[12]

As of 1937, Nina Shvangiradze, Georgian Latvian lady, was hired as a secretary (Strategic Services Unit, DB#1245, p.4; Kuromiya & Mamoulia, 2016, p.148) and couple of other local personals for housekeeping duties e.g. Zelma (housekeeper), Luize Kindelo (cook, Estonian), and Marie (nurse, Estonian).In this new location, they were able to borrow three rooms, one for Onodera's personal office, one for his family, and the last one for the office of Shvangiradze. The Baznīcas office was inherited by the successors of Onodera and remained until 1940, the year of the Soviet occupation of Latvia. After the Soviet annexation of Latvia in August 1940, the Riga army office was forced to be close down alongside the Japanese Legation. Already in June, the Soviet occupation forces attempted to arrest Nina

[12] There could be an additional reason for the choice of the location. Kisaburo Yokoi, Japanese merchant who is famous for opening the first store of Japanese goods in Moscow, had lived in Riga around that time and his shop was located in Brivibas iela 55, where was in the neighbourhood of Baznīcas iela.

Shvangiradze upon the invasion to Latvia and soon after, she married an American Legation staff (Onodera, 2016, p.183) and fled to Cairo. (Kuromiya & Mamoulia, 2016, p.148) On the other hand, Marie, Estonian nurse, was the one who escaped to Sweden like thousands of her own nationals. She worked for Japanese army office in Stockholm and again, served for Onodera who returned as a military attaché to Sweden in 1941. (Okabe, 2012, p.305)

Figure 5. Apartments in *Elizabetes iela* 33 (p.13) and *Baznīcas iela* 19 (p.14) in Riga, Latvia. (February 2017)

Figure 6. The house register of *Baznīcas iela* 19 building (1937-1940)

Major Onodera is listed as the residents along with the two housekeepers (Valentine Jillnets, a housemaid worked temporarily from May 1937 to April 1938, and the aforementioned Luize Kindelo) Courtesy: Latvian State Historical Archive (LVVA)

3. Position of 'Military Attaché to Latvia' in the Japanese Army

There were eight Japanese military officers served as military attachés to Latvia throughout the Interwar period. (see ***Appendix***) Among them, six had actually resided in Riga from 1931 to 1940. The aforementioned Colonel Suzuki and Major Hikosaburo Hata, the 2nd military attaché to Latvia from 1930 to 1931 (Tokyo Asahi Shimbun, April 9th 1943, p.1), administered Latvia from Warsaw and never moved to Riga.

Figure 7. Lieutenant Colonel Hikosaburo Hata (first from the right), probably during his term in office as a military attaché to the Soviet Union (1934-1936), at the Estonian General Staff in Tallinn. (1935) Courtesy: Estonian Film Archive (*Eesti filmiarhiiv*)

In July 1931, Major Osato Kawamata was appointed as the first military attaché in Riga residence. (Latvijas Kareivis, July 21st 1931, p.1).

There are no sources left for the details of his activities in Riga, but his term of office in Riga exactly collided with the most politically difficult period for the Interwar Baltic States hence it was presumably impossible to promote any intelligence works other than building friendship with Latvian military personals and other foreign military attachés.

Amidst economic panic and political unrests during the Great Depression, extreme right-wing parties emerged in the Baltic States such as the Association of Estonian Freedom Fighters (*Vabadussõjalaste Liit*) in Estonia and the Fire Cross (*Ugunkrusts*) in Latvia. While the governments of the Baltic States concentrated on political conflicts rather than tackling on the Depression, they attempted to take power by coup detat. (Von Rauch, 1974, p.148-152). As these extreme right-wingers were serious threats to the domestic securities which involved the nation's military forces, the Baltic governments took pre-emptive actions to clash their attempts including arrests of perpetrators and ban on their street marches. In order to avoid occurrence of similar organizations, the Baltic States installed 'authoritarian democracy' starting from 1934, which was somehow similar to many of European fascist regimes in later years. Ironically, the creation of strong governments brought back the political stabilities to the Baltic States.

Figure 8. Portrait of Major Osato Kawamata given as a present to Colonel Kikkuls, Head of the Latvian Intelligence Service. (July 1933?) Courtesy: Museum of the Occupation of Latvia (*Latvijas Okupācijas muzejs*)

The MoA should had recognized the geopolitical importance of Riga in terms of the intelligence against the Soviet Union because it had been repeatedly told by the diplomats like Ueda and their fellow officers e.g. Komatsubara. Still, as of early 1930s, there seems no attempts were made to station officers who specialized in intelligence activities. After Kawamata, who transferred to Moscow as a military attaché to the Soviet, Cavalry Lieutenant Colonel Tsutomu Ouchi succeeded the position. Ouchi was a cavalry professional but did not have expertise in intelligence operations. Indeed, the U.S. Onodera report says, Ouchi had sent only 40 telegrams to Tokyo from 1933 to 1935 (SSU, 1946, p.24) and based on the records of the correspondence available at the NIDS (Ministry of Defence) archive in Tokyo, 10 of them were regarding the exchange of weapons with the Estonian army in 1935, which will be explained later. Yet, as being the expert on cavalry operations (he became an instructor of the army's cavalry school after the return to Japan), he frequently visited the units of both the Estonian and Latvian armies and frankly exchanged opinions on the operations with the local officers.

Figure 9. Party of Japanese and Latvian Armies, probably taken at the Japanese Legation in *Jura Alunana iela* 2, Riga.(1934?) Courtesy: Museum of the Occupation of Latvia (*Latvijas Okupācijas muzejs*)

Around 1935, when Ouchi left Latvia, the internal strife among Japanese army, between the Imperial Way faction (*Kodouha*) and the Control faction (*Toseiha*), was intensified. Starting from the murder of General Tetsuzan Nagata on August 12th 1935, Executive Secretary of Military Affairs Bureau of the MoA who belonged to the latter faction, by Lieutenant Aizawa sympathized with the former faction; the political atmosphere surrounding Japanese army became so delicate. It was October 12th 1935 when Infantry Major Makoto Onodera assigned to be a next military attaché to Latvia. Already at the beginning of 1930s, Onodera was widely known as an expert of Russian military affairs in the army through his mature knowledge on the issue and speaking fluent Russian language.

He was most inspired by General Toshiro Obata who was one of the central figures of the Imperial Way faction. (Okabe, 2014, p.56) Obata and his fellows developed an unified critical feeling against the Soviet Union which re-emerged militarily after the success of the 'Five Years Plan' (1928-32). Thus, the strategic question 'how to defeat the Soviet military forces pre-emptively before the completion of another military expansion' became their focus. Fortunately, their ambitious war plan was never realized as the faction itself lost influence over the army, especially by the February 26 incident of 1936, a failed coup attempt by young officers of the Imperial Way faction. Many scholars including Okabe believe that Onodera was 'relegated' to Riga by the pressure of the Control faction members in an attempt to weaken their counterpart.

Indeed, Onodera himself stated the Riga army office a 'police box in the hinterland' (Okabe, 2012, p.105) Yet, from 1936 to 1938, Onodera had sent over 200 telegrams to Tokyo. (SSU, 1946, p.24) This appears to be true because of the existence of his 141st telegram sent from Riga on December 13th 1937, reporting the liquidation of the two Soviet generals to the MoA. (JACAR, Ref.C01004397400) In Latvia, and also in Estonia where he jointly administrated from 1937, he made a great success in the development of Japanese military intelligence activities in the Baltic States. The most notable case was the joint Estonian-Japanese military intelligence operations to topple the Soviet regimes in Eastern Europe of which Onodera took an initiative of. During his term in office, the Riga army office finally met the expectation of the MoA (or even more than that) in which the purpose to send officers to Latvia was the information gathering on the Soviet military affairs ever since the researchers in 1920s.

Cavalry Lieutenant Colonel Tamotsu Takatsuki, who succeeded Onodera's position in May 1938, was a specialist of 'field operations', according to the unpublished memoir of Makoto Onodera. Little is known or can be assumed with regard to his activities in Riga from the materials left, but the U.S. Onodera report tells he sent 300 telegrams to Tokyo in a year from 1938 to 1939. (SSU, 1946, p.24) In that sense, he was quite successful in terms of maintaining the Onodera's operations. In June 1939, only a year after, Takatsuki was replaced by Artillery Lieutenant Colonel Hiroshi Onouchi. Onouchi became the last Japanese military attaché to Latvia, by the Soviet occupation of the Baltic States in June 1940.

Figure 10. Portrait of Lieutenant Colonel Tamotsu Takatsuki given as a gift to Latvian Colonel Gregorijs Kikkuls. (1939)
Courtesy: Museum of the Occupation of Latvia (*Latvijas Okupācijas muzejs*)

To sum up, the histories of the Riga army office and Japanese military attachés to Latvia can be categorized into two periods: 1) 'Normal military attaché's office' (referred by Onodera as a 'Police box in the Hinterland') from 1931 to 1936, and 2) 'Hub for Japanese Military Intelligence Activities against the Soviet Union' from 1937 to 1940.

5. Visit of Captain Shimanuki to Estonia (1933-1934)

On November 25th 1933, Aviation Captain Tadamasa Shimanuki of the Japanese army arrived in Estonia from the Soviet Union. (Sakala, March 10th 1934, p.2). Prior to the visit to Estonia, he had researched 'Air and Ground Separation Theory' (also known as '*Kuuchi Bunri-Ron*' in Japanese) at the Soviet Air Force unit stationed in Ivanovo-Voznesensk (current Ivanovo), northeast of Moscow, from June 1932 (JACAR, Ref.B13091661400).

The first priority of him in Estonia was to research the flight condition in a season of severe cold. (Shimanuki, 1988, p. 111). On January 10th 1934, he entered the service at the 3rd flying division (Tallinn) of the Estonian Air Force. However, it was impossible to conduct such research there because of a mild winter 'once in three decades' and the bad conditions of the airfield. Still, by special grace of the division commander, Shimanuki was able to fly over Tallinn at least three or four times.

As being a rare guest from Japan, Shimanuki was interviewed by '*Sõdur*' (Soldier), official magazine of the Estonian Defence Forces, in the same month he arrived Estonia. The topic of the interview was about 'Japanese mentality' (Sakala, January 14th 1935, p.2: Sõdur, March 3rd 1934, p.250).
Also, at the 3rd flying division, Shimanaki was often visited by Estonian officers and was questioned about Japanese culture. In his letters to the family in Japan, Shimanuki described the characteristics of Estonians as follow:
"The characteristic of Estonians are really similar to that of Japanese. I found it delectable that they are really open-minded despite the lack of knowledge on (social) manners."

Before leaving the country, Shimanuki held his farewell reception at hotel '*Rooma*' (Rome) and enjoyed a pleasant talk with three generals belonged to the Estonian general staff such as Gustav Jonson, Johannes Roska (Orasmaa), and Juhan Tõrvand. (Lääne Teataja, March 10th 1934, p.3). On March 4th, Shimanuki was given the Estonian Order of the Cross of the Eagle (*Kotkaristi teenetemärk*) at the headquarters of Estonian Defence League (*Kaitseliit*) in Tallinn. (Shimanuki, 1988, p.111). Two days later, on the 6th, he left Tallinn for Torun (Poland), the last destination of his study trip in Europe.

The Estonian hospitality shown to Shimanuki was highly appreciated by the MoFA and the MoA. It became one of the reasons why the MoFA sought to promote the Chargé d'affaires of the Riga Legation to Envoy Extraordinary and Plenipotentiary. (JACAR, Ref. B14090839400) In late 1934, the MoFA demanded a budget in order for the Chargé d'affaires in Riga to administrate Estonia and Lithuania, however, this was denied by the MoF. Likewise, the MoA was also eager to promote the military attaché in Riga in the same way. But, as long as the military attaché was a part of the Riga Legation and in case, was also required to submit formal 'credentials' issued by the MoFA to the governments of Estonia and Lithuania, the plan had to be abolished. It had to wait until 1937 when the issue was took up again by then military attaché Makoto Onodera.

Figure 11. Captain Tadamasa Shimanuki[13] (third from the left, first row) at his farewell

[13] In 1939, Tadamasa Shimanuki participated in the battle of Khalkhin Gol (Nomonhan) as a chief of operations of the 2nd Flying Corps of the Kwantung Army. On July 3rd, he was killed in action while being on

reception in Hotel '*Rooma*' (Rome), Tallinn. (March 5th 1934)
Courtesy: Mr. Takamitsu Shimanuki (the excerpt from the book 'Memorial Writings for Tadamasa Shimanuki', published in 1988)

6. Exchange of Firearms between Estonian and Japanese Armies (1935)

In February 1935, an Estonian military delegation visited the Japanese Army office in Riga and had an opportunity to talk with the military attaché Tsutomu Ouchi, Cavalry Lieutenant Colonel. They agreed on an exchange of weapons to commemorate the beginning of the official relationship. (JACAR, Ref. C01004065200). In May, a Type 97 Sniper Rifle (indicated as 'Type 38 Infantry Rifle with Sniping Scope' in the official document), a Nambu Experimental Sub-Machinegun Type 2, and a Nambu Type 14 Handgun were presented to the Estonian Army.(JACAR, Ref. C01006736600). Except for the famous Nambu Pistol, the guns were all experimental weapons, which at that time were still on trial. Ouchi probably did not expect the Estonians to request the sort of weapons for the exchange and it would have been an even greater surprise for the MoA in Tokyo. In fact, on February 21st, the Ministry suddenly ordered the immediate acquirement of a Nambu Sub-Machinegun for the Technological Institute. (JACAR, Ref.C01006653500)

reconnaissance flight over Hailaer river. According to the post-war article of Takeharu Shimanuki, his younger brother who also participated in the battle, the plane was shot down by the Soviet anti-aircraft guns, of which around twenty were stationed in the area back then.

Figure 12. Lieutenant Colonel Tsutomu Ouchi (first from the left, second row) at the Latvian 1st Cavalry Regiment (*Latvijas 1. Jātnieku pulks*) in Daugavpils. (April 1935)
Courtesy: Latvian War Museum (*Latvijas Kara Muzejs)*

From May to June, fifty 6.5mm bullets for the Arisaka M1905 and one-hundred 8mm Nambu bullets were delivered to Estonia. (JACAR, Ref. C01004067100). In June, five-hundred Nambu bullets were additionally brought to Riga by Lieutenant Colonel Osato Kawamata, Military Attaché to the Japanese Embassy in Moscow, who used to be Ouchi's superior at the Riga Legation until July 1933. (JACAR, Ref. C01006855500)

Around this time, a modernization project of the existing weapons was ongoing in the *Arsenal*, Estonia's national firearms factory. Over 10,000 Japanese-made Arisaka M1905 rifles remaining in the Estonia Army were converted to 7.7mm British.303 from the original 6.5mm. There were three different sources for the Estonian Arisakas: 1) A surplus of Ex-Russian Imperial Army rifles purchased from Japan in 1915 by General Eduard Karlovich Germonius, 2) As part of the Finnish military aid given during the Estonian Independence War from December 1918 to January 1919, and 3) Those inherited from the Ex-Russian White Army led by Nikolai Nikolayevich Yudenich (only a few). In 1920s, around ten-twenty

Arisakas were additionally imported from the United Kingdom. The modernized Arisakas were transferred from the Estonian Army to new user, Estonian Defence League (*Kaitseliit*), the nation's official para-military organization. The larger clips for British.303 sometimes caused malfunctions in loading and ejecting, but otherwise it was a very powerful weapon which met the needs of the defence league soldiers.

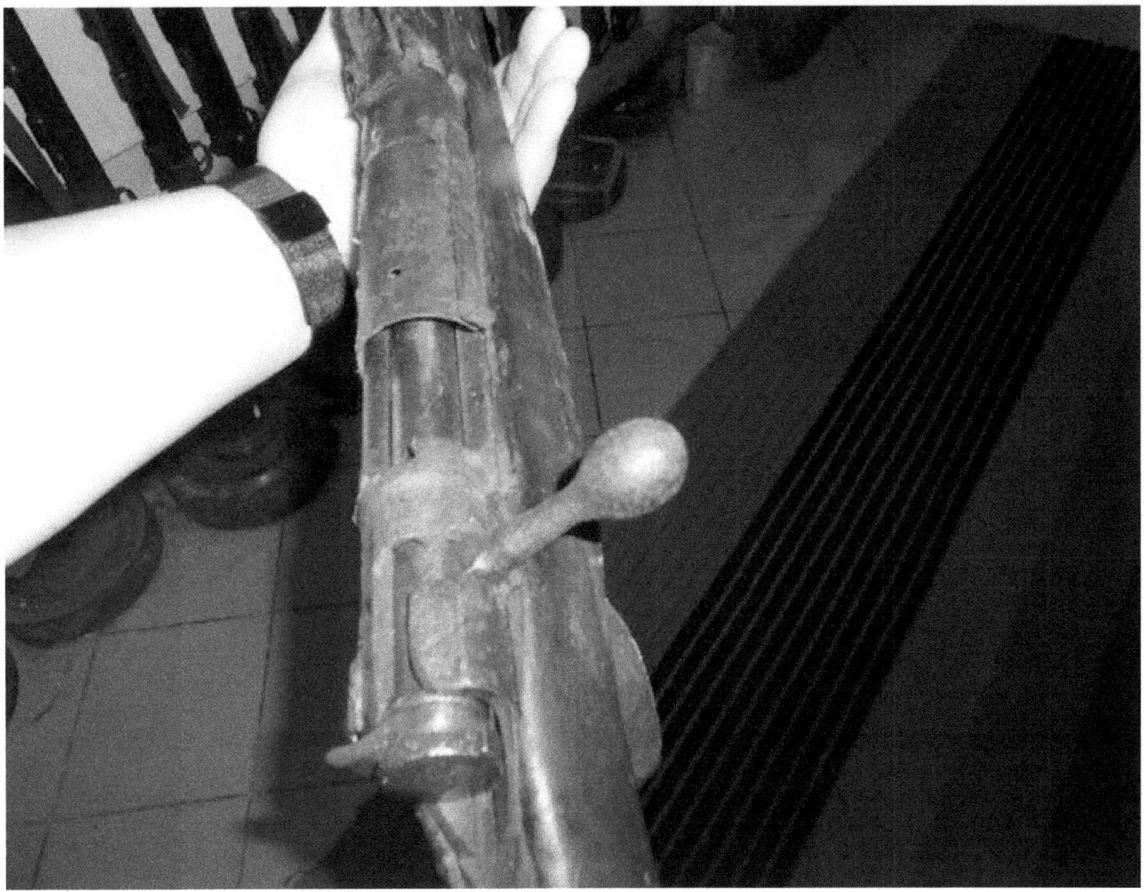

Figure 13. British.303-converted Arisaka M1905 at the Museum of Fight for Estonia's Freedom (*Eesti vabadusvõitluse museum*), Tallinn. (August 2014)

From the Estonian side, at least one Arsenal M23, the first Estonian-made sub-machinegun developed by the *Arsenal* in 1926, was sent to Japan via the Riga Legation. The Arsenal M23 was basically an Estonian imitation of the Bergmann MP18, a German sub-machinegun used during the Great War, but it was slightly improved in some ways. The Estonian imitation model was probably a technological 'milestone' for the developers themselves, but was completely obsolete by the time it was presented to the Japanese. In 1938, all the M23s were replaced by the Finnish-made Suomi KP/31 and the remainder were completely sold off to the Latvian Army and the Republican forces during the Spanish Civil War.

Unfortunately, the guns given as a gift from Japanese did not contribute to the Estonian development of firearms either, for two reasons, 1) The Estonia's spontaneous firearms development projects were cancelled due to the purchase of the latest Finnish guns. This was related to the attempts of Estonian-Finnish defence cooperation in the late 1930s and 2) The guns were somewhat obsolete from the perspective of the European standard of firearms. For example, the Type 97 Sniper Rifle guaranteed high accuracy rate with an advanced scope and a handmade barrel; it was a masterpiece of Japanese craftsmanship, but its ammunition was still weaker 6.5mm. According to Mr. Toe Nõmm of Estonian Defence Ministry, the three Japanese guns were probably seized by the Soviet occupation forces in either August or September 1940 and sent to the Soviet Union. However, no information regarding the whereabouts of the Arsenal M23 were found in either Japan or the Soviet-seized Japanese guns.

In late 1935, Ouchi returned to Japan, while being promoted to Colonel. He later worked as an instructor of the Army's cavalry school. In Summer 1939, upon the outbreak of the border conflict with the Soviet Union in Khalkhin Gol (*Nomonhan*), he was mobilized as a Chief of Staff of the 23rd Division led by General Michitaro Komatsubara.[14] On July 4th, while commanding retreating troops on a riverbank of Hailaer after the failed offensive, he was coincidentally killed by a Soviet shrapnel shell. (Yomiuri Shimbun, January 13th 1975, p.5)

7. The 7th World Comintern Congress and the German-Japanese Anti-Comintern Pact (1935-1936)

The transfer of the command of the Japanese military intelligence operations in Europe against the Soviet Union from the Warsaw army office to the Berlin army office happened upon the conclusion of the German-Japanese Anti-Comintern Pact on November 25th 1936.

The most likely cause of this 'crustal movement' was one of the resolutions adopted by the 7th World Congress of the Comintern (July-August 1935). It was named the 'Resolution of Tactics of the Anti-Fascism Popular Front' and called the unification of Chinese resistance between the Chinese Communist Party and

[14] The same person who was sent to Estonia on special mission between 1919-20. Kuromiya (2011) suggests General Komatsubara, who was probably a Soviet spy, assassinated Ouchi and concealed the crime. Yet, lacking the sources, this is nothing more than a conspiracy theory.

Kuomintang against Japanese Imperialism. Also, in the statement, Germany, Italy, and Japan were clearly indicated as 'Imperialist nations' which must be overthrown by the efforts of the world's communists. (Yomiuri Shimbun, July 14th 1972, p.21) Consequently, the statement was identified as a threat to Japanese management of Manchukuo and it was reported to Tokyo by Captain Etsuo Kotani, assistant military attaché of Japanese Embassy in Moscow. (Yomiuri Shimbun, February 16th 1971, p.21) Ironically, the Comintern resolution only worked in the way strengthening German-Japanese diplomatic tie.

However, Lieutenant Colonel Onodera, Japanese military attaché of the Riga Legation, doubted the actual Soviet military strength. Thanks to the friendship with Nikolai Reek, then Chief of the Estonian General Staff, he gained information regarding the vulnerabilities of the Soviet military forces. In the telegram sent by Onodera to Vice Chief of Staff in Tokyo on June 20th 1936, he reported the vulnerabilities as follows: 1) the recent expansion of the Soviet military forces does not mean the improvement in its quality, 2) the Soviet military equipment, especially automobiles and airplanes, are run by 'imported' parts. And, upon his return to Japan on May 28st 1938, Onodera told the Japan Times that 'Soviet is no menace to a strong Japan' due to the lack of 'military preparedness' on the Soviet side. (The Japan Times, May 30th 1938, p.1)

Anyway, Germans and 'mainstream' Japanese military attachés were thinking differently. In Berlin, Friedrich Hack, German arms broker with pro-Nazi tendency, visited the Japanese Army office in Berlin as a messenger of Joachim von Ribbentrop either in May or June 1935 and he proposed a bilateral military alliance tackling the Soviet ambitions to Major General Hiroshi Oshima, then military attaché. (Yomiuri Shimbun, July 12th 1972, p.21) According to Oshima, prior to the German offer, he spontaneously proposed the bilateral alliance in the telegrams to Tokyo number of times. Anyway, Tokyo finally realized the effectiveness of the bilateral alliance with Germany, and signed the Anti-Comintern Pact with Germany in 1936.

Figure 14. Portrait of Estonian General Nikolai Reek sent to Major Takeharu Shimanuki, Japanese assistant military attaché stationed in Estonia, on September 30th 1938. Courtesy: National Institute for Defence Studies (NIDS) Archive, Tokyo. (Archival Reference: 島貫武治陸軍大佐戦前アルバム(防衛省防衛研究所所蔵 「中央全般写真 37・38」)

8. Joint Intelligence Operations against the Soviet Union (1937-1939)

By the late 1930s, the political situation in Europe descended into chaos due to the prolonged influences of the Great Depression, the Great Purge in the Soviet Union, and also the expansionism of Nazi Germany.

In January 1938, Major Makoto Onodera[15], Japanese Military Attaché in Riga, who also administrated Estonia and Lithuania ever since 1937, requested the detachment of additional personal for 'negotiations' with the Estonian military. (JACAR, Ref. C01004434500). A month later, Chargé d'affaires Hirata of Japanese Legation in Poland, answered Onodera's request by dispatching Infantry Captain Takeharu (Takeji) Shimanuki who belonged to his Legation.

Takeharu Shimanuki[16], who was actually the younger brother of the aforementioned Aviation Captain Tadamasa Shimanuki, worked for the Japanese Embassy in Moscow as the Army's official researcher for a year since April 1937 (JACAR, Ref. C01004299100) and at the time of being chosen as the liaison officer for Estonia, he was spending the last year of his researcher position in Europe at the Warsaw Legation. According to the memoir of Yuriko Onodera, wife of Lieutenant Colonel Onodera, Tokyo accepted their request because her husband's previous intelligence works were highly appreciated by them. (Onodera, 2007, p.53).

By the way, the reason why Onodera was in urgent need of the liaison officer was the ongoing Estonian-Japanese joint intelligence operation between 'Manaki Organ' (*Manaki Kikan*) of Japanese Army and Department 2 of the Estonian General Staff (*Sõjavägede Staabi II osakond*), Estonia's only foreign intelligence service back then. (Okabe, 2014, p.86: Strategic Services Unit, DB#1225, p.24). The former was secret intelligence organization of Japanese military attachés in

[15] Makoto Onodera returned to Japan on May 28th 1938. Two years later, in November 1940, he was appointed to military attaché to Sweden. In the post-war period, he worked as a Swedish translator along with his wife Yuriko. Passed from acute cardiac insufficiency on August 17th 1987. Aged 89.

[16] His residence in Tallinn was Pärnu maantee 20. He hired at least two Estonian ladies (one for secretary and the another for housekeeping duty)

Europe led by Infantry Colonel Takanobu Manaki[17], assistant army attaché of the Berlin Embassy. (Kuromiya & Mamoulia, 2016, p.174) Before 1937, all Japanese military intelligence operations in Northern and Eastern Europe were commanded by the army office in Warsaw.[18] However, upon the intensification of military cooperation with the Nazi Germany especially after the conclusion of the bilateral special agreements on joint intelligence operations in May 1937, its role was taken over by the Manaki Organ in the Berlin army office.[19] Levent (2012) found that the Manaki Organ was first established by Lieutenant Colonel Shigeki Usui[20] in 1937 and succeeded by Colonel Manaki in 1938. The organ had annually sent around 30 agents to Estonia, Finland, Lithuania, Poland and Turkey until 1939. (p.79-80)

Usui was actually school mates of Onodera from the Army Academy and the Army College, they knew each other quite well. Thus, it is rational to think Onodera told Usui about his special tie with the Estonian. By the way, despite its name, Manaki, the organ commander himself, probably did not have much contact with Onodera as he arrived to Europe in around early 1938, few months before Onodera heads back to Japan. This is one reason why Manaki is rarely mentioned in the Onodera's post-war memoirs. On the other hand, Usui had been stationed in Berlin ever since 1935 and was aware of the existence of Onodera in Riga.

There were basically two objectives in the joint Estonian and Japanese intelligence operations: 1) Toppling the Soviet regimes of Georgia and Ukraine by supporting independence movements of émigré activists and 2) Gathering political and military information of the Soviet Union by the penetrated Estonian agents. (Okabe, 2014, p.87: Kuromiya & Mamoulia, 2016, p.173). In the post-war memoir, Onodera mentioned about his connection with the government of Belarusian People's Republic (BPR) in exile, located in Prague, Czechoslovakia. (Onodera, 1992, p.35) He first gained a Belarusian informant in Riga, namely

[17] Takanobu Manaki (1894-1979).
[18] The Warsaw army office was located inside Japanese Legation (later promoted to Embassy) to Poland (Address: Foksal 10).
[19] JACAR, Ref.C01001775900
[20] Shigeki Usui (1898-1942).

Ezavitau, by using the connection of his secretary Shvangiradze.[21] (Onodera, 1992, p.35) And, through the network of émigré Belarusians, Onodera was able to make an acquaintance with Zacharka[22], the last BPR President, but denied any collaboration with them during the post-war SSU interrogations. In terms of the relations with the Belarusian nationalists, Onodera made a false representation to the Americans. He actually was eager to mobilize the Belarusian nationalists; however it was never realized since Japanese supports toward the Belarusian nationalists met strong Polish resistance. Onodera at least travelled to Wilno (current Vilnius)[23] twice (SSU, DB#1226, p.7) to contact Kozlov, the BPR supporter introduced from Ezavitov, but had to cancel future trips to the city due to the protest from 'Poland'.[24] (Onodera, 1992, p.35)

Meanwhile, Onodera contacted 'Adamowitch' (Adamowicz), leader of Polish secret organization in Danzig (current Gdansk). Thanks to Adamowitch and his fellows, Onodera found out the leak of official secrets regarding the ongoing secret intelligence operations. (Onodera, 1992, p.35) He immediately reported it to Lieutenant Colonel Usui in Berlin.[25]

Beginning from German requests regarding the status of Danzig (Gdansk) handed to Poland on October 24th 1938, an intimate relationship between Germany and Poland began to deteriorate. (Yamazaki, 2010, p.111) Indeed, the failure of Japanese intelligence operations targeting Belarus became obvious and there was no space for Japanese to intervene with the complicated Eastern European diplomatic issues.

With the failure of mobilizing the émigré activists, the Manaki Organ rather concentrated on penetrating their own agents to the Soviet Union. In 1938, to help

[21] The U.S. Onodera report (DB#1245) suggests that Shvangiradze had connected with DAMAT, Ukrainian nationalist organization based in Berlin. (p.3-4) This means the Interwar Belarussian, Georgian, and Ukrainian nationalist organizations were all intertwined.
[22] Vasil Zacharka (1877-1943), the second President of Belarusian People's Republic.
[23] Until the early 20th century, the city had been a 'philosophical Capital' for Belarusian nationalists.
[24] Onodera merely stated 'Poland', thus the opponent was most likely Polish government or its military, but it is rational to think the Warsaw army office also took a stand against the use of the Belarusians inside Poland.
[25] Professor Hiroaki Kuromiya of Indiana University claims Manaki's mistress in Paris, who was a Soviet NKVD agent, was involved in the leakage of the secret operations. However, Manaki arrived only few months before Onodera leaves Europe, thus it is highly unlikely that Onodera's discovery was linked to the mistress.

infiltrations of Estonian agents into the Soviet Union by a high-speed boat in Lake Peipsi, Onodera supplied 16,000 German Marks to Richard Maasing, Chief of the Estonian Intelligence Service.[26] From Estonian side, Lieutenant Colonel Villem (Wilhelm) Saarsen and Major Aksel Kristian were named as the liaison officers of the operations.[27] Villem Saarsen, the 'right-hand' man of Maasing, was an Estonian military attaché to Latvia (1934-1939) and actually the closest friend of Onodera in Riga.[28]

Figure 15. Major Makoto Onodera (fourth from the left, second row) at officer's club in

[26] In one of the U.S. reports, Onodera claimed he only provided the cash to the EIS, meanwhile, in the 'unpublished' memoir completed by 1992, which is currently preserved at the Yasukuni Archive in Tokyo, he stated "the construction of the boat was fully funded by Japanese and once it was completed in Germany, we handed the boat to Estonians".

[27] Professor Ivo Juurvee of Estonian national police academy (*Sisekaitseakadeemia*), who has an expertise in the Interwar Estonian military intelligence history, clearly denied the existence of such deal from one reason: the Soviet border security on Lake Peipsi throughout late 1930s was 'extremely weakened' due to the Great Purge hence there was no need for such special equipment to cross the border.

[28] Saarsen fled to Germany after the Soviet occupation of Estonia in 1940. And, after his house was burnt by the Allies air raid to Berlin in 1941, he moved to Stockholm and sought for the protection under the old friend Makoto Onodera who was a Japanese military attaché to Sweden. Throughout the war period, Saarsen worked as an informant for Onodera in Stockholm. In the post-war period, he became the political leader of the defected Estonians in Sweden. Onodera often visited him in Stockholm and kept exchanging letters until his death. Passed on January 29th 1982. Aged 90.

Riga. (March 30th 1937) There were also Latvian Colonel Gregorijs Kikkuls (third from the right, second row), Major Feliks Brzeskwinski (third from the left, second row), Polish military attaché to Latvia, and Lieutenant Colonel Villem Saarsen(fourth from the right, second row), Estonian military attaché to Latvia. Courtesy: Museum of the Occupation of Latvia (*Latvijas Okupācijas muzejs*)

Similarly, Onodera arranged cooperation with Colonel Gregolijs Ķikkuls[29], Chief of Latvian military intelligence service called the 'Information Department' (*Informacja dala*). (Strategic Services Unit, DB#1225, p.24). Yuriko, Onodera's wife, stated in her memoir that her husband provided only general information to Latvians, which were brought by Japanese diplomatic couriers arriving from Tokyo. The U.S. report indicated Onodera's tie with Berzins, Latvian interior minister. (Strategic Services Unit, DB#1225, p.24). But, overall, Latvians had never been recognized as 'good collaborators' by Onodera.

[29] Gregorijs Kikkuls (1888-1966). He was a Chief of the Information Department between 1934 and 1939, then became a military attaché to Poland and Romania from June 1939 and from October 1939, military attaché to Sweden and Norway. During the war, he remained in Stockholm and worked for the British secret service. Passed in England, 1966. Aged 78.

Figure 16. Portrait of Yuriko Onodera, given as a gift to the wife of Latvian Colonel Kikkuls. (March 1938) Courtesy: Museum of the Occupation of Latvia (*Latvijas Okupācijas muzejs*)

The estrangement between Onodera and Latvians was probably resulted from organizational structure of *Informacja dala* (Information Department of the Latvian General Staff, in which role and organizational scale were equivalent to that of the Estonian intelligence service). According to Juurvee (2003), number of intelligence officers in the Interwar Baltic States was limited. (Dozens of officers, approximately) While The Estonian intelligence service was originally designed to be suitable for information exchange with foreign military attachés, such mission was merely an additional task for the Latvian intelligence service. (p.47).

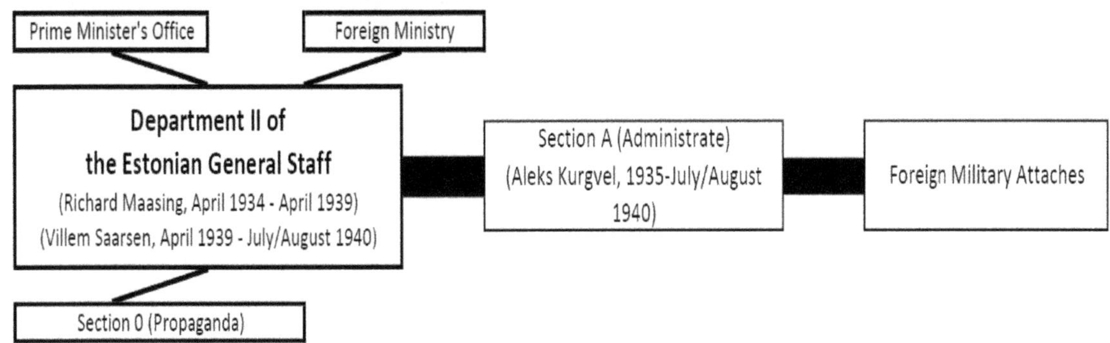

Figure 17. Organizational Structure of the Department II of the Estonian General Staff (*Sõjavägede Staabi II osakond*) in 1939. Based on 'Wartime Structure of the Estonian Army Intelligence' (*Eesti sõjaväeluure sõjaaegne struktuur*) - ERA f.495, n.12, s.113, I.139.

Unfortunately, Onodera could not confirm all the results since he returned to Japan on May 28th 1938 (Tokyo Asahi Shimbun, May 29th 1938, p.1), but the operations were taken over by Cavalry Lieutenant Colonel Tamotsu Takatsuki[30], new military attaché of the Riga Legation. (Strategic Services Unit, DB#1225, p.24). The U.S. Onodera report described Takatsuki as a 'capable person' equivalent to his predecessor. Also, he was known as a 'strategy expert' among the army. (Onodera, 1992, p.39) But, his job in Riga lasted only a year, shorter than any of the military attaches. With regard to the fact, Susumu Nishiura, ex-MoA adjutant general, provided an interesting fact that Takatsuki was a strong proponent of Japanese invasion of French Indochina (Nishiura, 2014, p.286), which became the immediate cause of the U.S. oil embargo on Japan, ultimately, the war between the two nations. Thus, he was probably found to be unsuitable for commanding the 'delicate' intelligence operations involving various nations.

[30] He returned to Japan on July 8th 1939 and soon after promoted to a staff officer of the General Staff of Japanese Army and in November 1940, transferred to Northern China Army HQ. But, on the 29th, Takatsuki was assassinated by anti-Japanese activists on the street of Beijing in broad daylight. (Tokyo Asahi Shimbun, December 1st 1940, p.1).

Figure 18. Lieutenant Colonel Tamotsu Takatsuki (first from the left) with Lieutenant Colonel Jacques Hoppenot, French military attaché to Latvia. (May 1938)
Courtesy: Museum of the Occupation of Latvia (*Latvijas Okupācijas muzejs*)

In July 1938, Shimanuki set up an office of Japanese military representative at Pärnu Beach Hotel (*Pärnu Rannahotell*). (Postimees, July 16th 1938, p.4). The Pärnu office remained for few weeks during the month. (Uus Eesti Pärnu Uudised, July 15th 1938, p.1). On September 30th 1938, after 7 months of the works under Onodera and Takatsuki, 'Major' Shimanuki[31] left Estonia for Japan. (JACAR, Ref.C01004593400).

[31] Takeharu Shimanuki, younger brother of the aforementioned Aviation Captain Tadamasa Shimanuki, was transferred to China after his return to Japan. He participated in the Battle of Khalkhin Gol (*Nomonhan*) in 1939 as a staff officer of the Kwantung Army, and at the end of the WW2 in 1945 he held the rank of Colonel. In the post-war period, he worked as the chief of the National Institute of Defence Studies (NIDS). Passed from pneumonia on December 20th 1978. Aged 76.

Figure 19. Major Takeharu Shimanuki (right end, first row) at the Legation of Japan in Helsinki, Finland. [32] (1938) Courtesy: National Institute for Defence Studies (NIDS) Archive, Tokyo. (Archival Reference: 島貫武治陸軍大佐戦前アルバム(防衛省防衛研究所所蔵「中央全般写真 37・38」)

[32] Chiune Sugihara (centre in the second line), who was a then chargé d'affaires to Finland and later became famous for saving thousands of Jewish refugees by issuing Japanese transit visa as an Acting Consul of Japanese Consulate in Kaunas, Lithuania, and Lieutenant Colonel Yoshihide Kato (Left of Shimanuki), then military attaché of the Legation (1936-1938), were also confirmed.

Figure 20. Pärnu maantee 20 building, Tallinn. (March 2017)

Major Takeharu Shimanuki lived in the fourth floor.

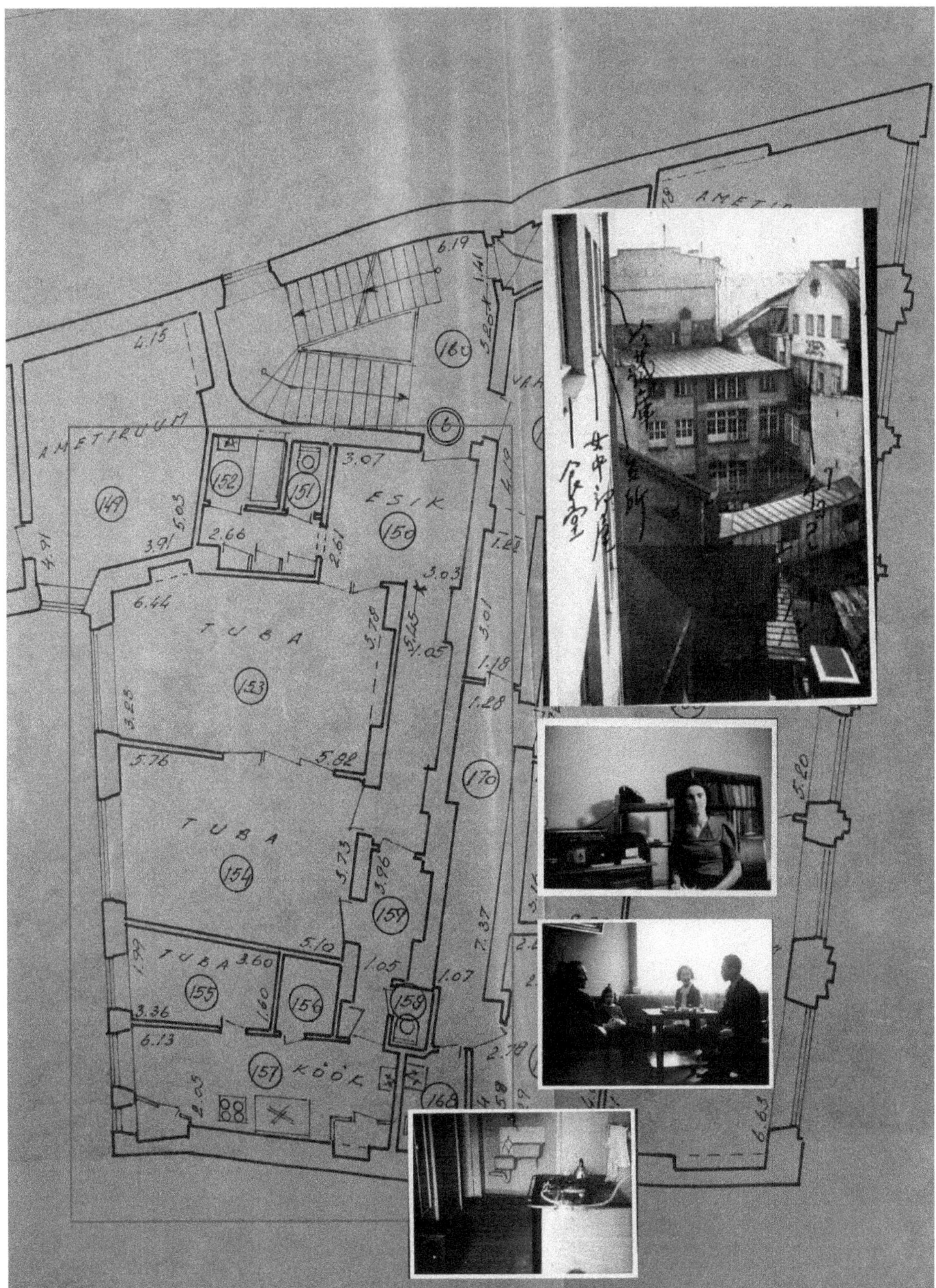

Figure 21. One Day at the Fourth Floor of Pärnu maantee 20 in 1938

Courtesy: (Architectural Drawing of Pärnu maantee 20) Tallinn City Archive (*Tallinna linnaarhiiv*) (Photos of Shimanuki at Pärnu maantee 20) National Institute for Defence Studies (NIDS) Archive, Tokyo. (Archival Reference: 島貫武治陸軍大佐戦前アルバム(防衛省防衛研究所所蔵 「中央全般写真 37･38」)

Figure 22. Major Takeharu Shimanuki (first from the right) among foreign military attachés at *Võidupüha* military parade in Tallinn (June 23rd 1938). Courtesy: Estonian Film Archive (*Eesti filmiarhiiv)*

The joint operations continued even after Shimanuki left Estonia. Despite the failure of the first objective, overthrowing the Soviet regimes, the second objective did succeed with certain achievements. For example, one Estonian agent worked for the Soviet General Staff (*Stavka*) kept providing general political and also some secret information of the Soviet Army until the arrest in the end of 1939. (Juurvee, 2013, p.38). Onodera was provided the information brought by the Estonian agent through the EIS, and in order to receive the secret information, he frequently travelled to Tallinn, more than once in a month. On December 13th 1937, he reported Tokyo that the two Latvian generals in the Soviet military forces 'Aratonis'[33] and 'Bokis' were purged and indicated the source of the

[33] Yakov Alksnis (1897-1938), Chief of Staff of the Soviet Air Force who was arrested on 23 November 1937 and expelled from the Communist party. Viktor Alksnis, current Duma (Russian parliament) member who is known

information as an 'agent'. (JACAR, Ref.C01004397400) This 'agent' was possibly the Estonian agent penetrated the Soviet General Staff as he was probably the only person who could afford such information.

The Estonian intelligence networks inside the Soviet Union grow dramatically throughout late 1930s, from Moscow to Eastern Siberia. In Volga region, the EIS used local ethnic Estonian colonies to collect information. According to Okabe (2014), the decision of using Estonian agents in East of Ural Mountain was actually based on the request of Japanese General Staff. (p.87) However, the Soviet was aware of the dangers of non-Russian ethnic minorities turning into foreign informants. And, their fears against 'anything foreign' amidst the Great Purge accelerated the plan to wipe out the century-long linguistic diversity of Siberia. In 1938, almost all schools in Siberia teaching in foreign languages, including two Estonian schools in the Altai region, were ordered to close down. (Hartley, 2014, p.230).

And, as none of the official documents after 1937 report the achievements of the EIS intelligence activities, it is rational to think the operations in East Siberia had failed at some point.

9. The Outbreak of the Second World War and the Soviet Expansionism

On September 1st 1939, Nazi Germany invaded Poland. Two days later, France and the United Kingdom declared war on Germany. It was the beginning of the Second World War.

The three Baltic States of Estonia, Latvia, and Lithuania jointly declared neutrality soon after the outbreak of the war, since their economy and military capabilities were never strong enough to provide a resistance against any of the great powers. Nevertheless, the effect of their neutrality was very limited in front of the Molotov-Ribbentrop Pact which promised partition of Central and Eastern Europe between the Soviet Union and Nazi Germany. In the secret protocol of the pact, the Baltic States were to be annexed by the Soviet Union.

---

for the close friendship with Masaru Sato, ex-Japanese diplomat specialized in Russian political affairs, is a grandson of him.

Shin Sakuma[34], the first Japanese Envoy Extraordinary and Plenipotentiary to Latvia, Estonia, and Lithuania since February 1937, summarized the speech of General Johan Laidoner, the Supreme Commander of the Estonian Defence Forces, in a diplomatic telegram sent to Foreign Minister Hirota on December 17th 1937 as '*Estonia has no foreign threats*' and '*Estonia does not rely on either Germany or the Soviet Union.*' It was not only Estonia but also the other two Baltic States proclaimed 'neutrality' in-between the two great powers. On the other hand, Estonia sought for military alliances with neighbouring states in case of next total war in Europe. However, those attempts, especially the 'Baltic alliance' with Latvia did not succeed for some reasons such as German political intervention (Germans were pretending to be a supporter of the Baltic States on the other hand attempted to break off the ties between Estonians and Latvians – according to Ilmjärv) and the historical rivalry between Estonia and Latvia. For example, the Estonian-Latvian military alliance was actually formalized on November 1st 1923. (Ilmjärv, 2003, p.89) But, they could not overcome the distrusts ever since the medieval age thus this first-ever Baltic military alliance was torn apart by early 1930s. Afterward, Estonia strengthened military cooperation with Finland and Poland throughout late 1930s, which were rather stronger neighbours with less controversial historical backgrounds compared to Latvia.

The peace in the Baltic States lasted only few weeks. On September 14th 1939, the Polish submarine '*Orzeł*' entered the military port in Tallinn and was interned due to the Estonian neutrality, but it soon escaped. The Soviet Union claimed the submarine sunk their tanker '*Metalist*' in Estonian territorial water on the 17th (Yomiuri Shimbun, September 29th 1939, p.1) and soon after, on the 24th, they demanded Estonia to accept the immediate stationing of Red Army troops. (Kasekamp, 2010, p.125). In order to avoid a worst scenario, the Estonian government had no other choice but to accept the demand. The rest of the Baltic

[34] Envoy Shin Sakuma returned to Japan on November 14th 1938 by Japanese ocean liner *Terukuni-Maru*. Later, he came back to Europe as a personal adviser of Oshima Hiroshi, the Ambassador to Nazi Germany, and was formerly appointed as the Envoy Extraordinary and Plenipotentiary to Nazi Germany on February 18th 1941. After the war, he volunteered as a defence counsel for Oshima, who was charged as a Class-A war criminal in the Tokyo Tribunal. Passed on December 8th, 1987. Aged 94.

States also received the same demands from the Soviet Union within next few months and lacking the supports of any of the nearby great powers (Germany remained neutral in this matter due to the secret agreement of the Molotov-Ribbentrop Pact but ordered the repatriation of all the Baltic Germans to Germany), there was no way to resist against it.

In the Riga Legation, with the resignation of Sakuma (described as an 'honourable retirement' on Japanese newspapers) in December 1938, Shojiro Ohtaka[35] was appointed as his successor. Also, after the return of Takatsuki to Japan, Artillery Lieutenant Colonel Hiroshi Onouchi[36] succeeded his position in June 1939.

Figure 23. Envoy Shojiro Ohtaka (sitting in left) at the Ceremony of the Presentation of Credentials to Estonian President Konstantin Päts (sitting in centre) on June 20th 1939.

[35] Envoy Shojiro Ohtaka obeyed the order to return to Japan issued on August 12th 1940, then, was forced to resign from the MoFA in October due to the personal reduction. He passed in 1966. Aged 74.

[36] Onouchi became a military attaché to Finland in September 1940, after the Soviet occupation of Latvia. At the end of the WW2, he was the Chief of the 53rd Army stationed in Japan, at the rank of Major General. Passed on August 21st 1984. Aged 84.

Lieutenant Colonel Hiroshi Onouchi[37], military attaché of the Riga Legation, is standing behind Ohtaka. Courtesy: Estonian Film Archive (*Eesti filmiarhiiv*)

In July 1939, General Torashiro Kawabe, Japanese military attaché to Nazi Germany made three days trip to Estonia. He used to be the Army researcher in Riga, in 1920s, and due to his outstanding intelligence skills and knowledge in the Soviet military affairs, Tokyo assigned Kawabe as a new commander of the Manaki Organ. According to the memoir of Saarsen published in 1978, throughout the Interwar period, Kawabe used to travel around Europe to supervise Japanese Army Attachés stationed in each countries. (Saarsen, 1978, p.184).

On the first day when Kawabe arrived to Tallinn from Berlin, Saarsen took him to Viimsi Manor in Jõelähtme Parish where was the permanent residence of General Johan Laidoner, Commander-in-chief of the Estonian Army. (Saarsen, 1978, p.184-185). The three officers, Kawabe, Laidoner, and Saarsen frankly exchanged opinions about the political situations of Europe, especially German intensions, on private beach near the Manor. While Kawabe was seeing the whole situation rather opportunistic, relying on the wisdom of European politicians to avoid the second total war, Laidoner gave a pessimistic answer to him that the war in Europe is inevitable. (Saarsen, 1978, p.186) Although Saarsen stated the details of the conversation very ambiguously, Kawabe detailed it in his memoir as follow: "General Laidoner said, 'the most unpleasant thing for me is Polish jingoism. Such attitude will result in another historic tragedy. Furthermore, their tragedy leads to our tragedy." (Kawabe, 1962, p.101) Eventually, Laidoner's concern was materialized in only few months time from this highly political session with the Japanese general.

Next day, Kawabe travelled from Tallinn to Narva, and then continued to Narva-Jõesuu, Estonia's Eastern border towns. In Narva-Jõesuu, Captain Aleks (Aleksei) Kurgvel, Chief of Section A of the Estonian Intelligence Service, joined lunch at restaurant 'Villa Capriccio'. (Uus Eesti, July 4th 1939, p.5). Indeed, this small

[37] He lost the Estonian contacts inherited from Onodera and Takatsuki after moving to Helsinki. However, another contact, Estonian Admiral Johan Pitka, who later became the leader of the Estonian voluntary corps during the Soviet re-occupation in 1944, kept providing him information regarding the political situations in Estonia under the Soviet occupation. He survived the war and passed on August 21st 1984. Aged 84.

border town was popular among Estonian and Japanese intelligence officers. Later in the same month, Hiroshi Sugawara, military attaché of the Moscow Embassy, visited Narva-Jõesuu with his wife and enjoyed taking pictures of 'surroundings'. (Uus Eesti, July 15th 1939, p.6). So to say, their trip to the region was to observe the Soviet border defence and to exchange the information frankly.

Figure 24. Estonian-Russian border in Narva. (August 2014)

After the two border towns, the group stopped in Kiviõli, an industrial town in Ida-Viru country, Eastern Estonia where was famous for shale oil mining. (Uus Eesti, July 4th 1939, p.3). Saarsen wrote, "Mines (in Kiviõli) caught great attentions from the Japanese officers. They were all ears and eyes on everything they hear and see there". (Saarsen, 1978, p.188). In the same month, the United States handed a denunciation of the U.S.-Japanese Treaty of Commerce and Navigation to Japan due to the intensification of its aggressions over China. On July 28th, Ambassador Horiuchi to the U.S. reported Foreign Minister Arita that "Since the U.S. is the only market to fulfil Japan's needs on oil, silk, and iron scrap, (in case of total embargo), it will definitely make Japan's military actions in China impossible." (MoFA, 2011, Volume 3, p.2283-2284).

Kawabe's trip to Estonia did not have any influences on the Japanese military intelligence activities in the Baltic States, but highlighted the difference in perception of 'threats' between Estonia and Japan. Laidoner indicated the Polish jingoism as the possible cause of next war in Europe, but Kawabe had been taken the Nazi expansionism as a serious threat to the post-WW1 pacifism in Europe. In both Saarsen and Kawabe's memoirs, the reaction of Kawabe to the opinion of Laidoner is never introduced. It is not clear whether Kawabe was afraid of provoking the Estonian hero or just pretended to be 'diplomatic' as much as possible, but Kawabe's suspicion over Japan's inclinations to Nazism and Nazi Germany was identical for the Berlin Embassy staffs. Then Ambassador Hiroshi Oshima to Nazi Germany (1938-1945) was known for dragging off Shigenori Togo, his predecessor with pro-Jewish tendency, from the seat of the Ambassador in 1938 when he was a military attaché to the Berlin Embassy. Oshima's personality was lunatic, he had completely intoxicated with Nazism and Kawabe had been in strife with him. It is said Kawabe yelled at Oshima upon the conclusion of the Molotov-Ribbentrop Pact in August 1939, blaming his incompetence as a diplomat, and took an initiative of discharging Oshima from his position. Soon after the Oshima's dismissal, Kawabe himself was also called back to Tokyo in Autumn 1939. (Kawabe, 1962, p.102)

In October 1939, with the help of Feliks Brzeskwinski, Polish military attaché to Latvia (1933-1940) whom Onodera and his family previously had close friendship, the Polish army intelligence officer Michał Rybikowski arrived to Riga from the occupied Poland. Onouchi hired him as an informant, according to the advice of Brzeskwinski, and Rybikowski was given a new identity as Manchukuo citizen named 'Heita Iwanobe' (from his codename 'Iwanov'). (Okabe, 2014, p.131)

Ever since the Soviet stationing of its military forces to the Baltic States (October-November 1939), the local military intelligence services including the Estonian

'Department 2' began to take a distance from Onouchi. Thus, the connection with Rybikowski became the most precise ever in terms of gaining the Soviet information. Indeed, there were two Polish agents in Narva (the Estonian-Soviet border town) and as Onouchi's friendship with the Baltic intelligence services were deteriorating, the Polish intelligence organs must had been the only 'trustful' source of the information.

Still, around this period, Onouchi probably maintained good relationship with some of the few officers of the Baltic military forces, who were the aforementioned Aksel Kristian of the Estonian intelligence service and Colonel Gregolijs Kikkuls, then Latvian military attaché to Nordic countries who used to be a head of the Latvian intelligence service. For instance, before the Soviet occupation of the Baltic States, in exchange for the Soviet information provided by the Estonian intelligence service, he provided them some money equivalent to 500 Japanese Yen monthly, first in British Pounds and later in the U.S. Dollars. (Strategic Services Unit, DB#1225, p.27)

Figure 25. Lieutenant Colonel Hiroshi Onouchi (left), then Japanese military attaché to the Baltic States (1939-1940), and Michal Rybikowski (right).
Courtesy: (Photo of Onouchi) Mr. Ronny Rönnqvist, Chairman of the Japanese Cultural Association in Finland. (Photo of Rybikowski) Department of History, Polish Ministry of

Defence (*Wojskowe Biuro Historyczne*)

10. The Soviet Invasion of the Baltic States and the Fate of the Japanese Diplomatic Missions

On June 16th 1940, when the eyes of the world were concentrated on Germany's entry into Paris, the Soviet Union finally began to invade Estonia and Latvia. The Soviet operation against Lithuania was launched a day before. By the 23rd, the Soviet army completed the occupation of all the three nations.

As the Kremlin anticipated, the news of the Soviet invasion of the Baltic States was obscured by the German victory over France. With less attention being shown by the world regarding the occupation, the Soviet implemented its next objective. This was the installation of pro-Soviet regimes in the Baltic States to legitimize the occupation. Street demonstrations were frequently held by the local communist activists and to solidify the occupation, Andrei Zhdanov, a Soviet Politburo member was sent to Tallinn. (Kasekamp, 2010, p.128). With pressure from the Soviet-backed Communists and the Red army, the Baltic governments decided to call general elections on July 14th and 15th.

In the general election in Estonia, candidates of the Soviet-backed 'Worker's Union' surprisingly gained a majority in the *Riigikogu* (Parliament), with a 99.9% approval rate. (Tokyo Asahi Shimbun, July 19th 1940, p.3). Unquestionably, the result of the election itself and the approval rate were already fabricated by the Soviet Union before the actual voting started. The new Communist administration did not meet any resistance when they voted for Estonia becoming part of the Soviet Union. The Estonian request for the annexation on the 21st was immediately accepted by the Supreme Soviet in Moscow. (Kasekamp, 2010, p.129).

On August 11th, the Soviet Foreign Minister, Vyacheslav Mikhailovich Molotov, officially declared the Soviet annexation of the Baltic States and demanded the diplomatic missions in the region to leave by the 25th, which was the expiration date of their credentials to the former governments.

Amid the confusion, the MoFA issued an order for the return of Envoy Ohtaka on August 12th. He obeyed the order but for that reason, the negotiations with the Soviet authority became even more difficult. On September 5th, the Riga Legation was finally closed alongside other two Japanese diplomatic missions in the Baltic States (Diplomat office in Tallinn, Estonia and Consulate in Kaunas, Lithuania).

While the Legation members fled to Berlin, military attaché Onouchi instead chose Stockholm, Sweden as his destination. (Okabe, 2014, p.131: JACAR, Ref.C13070990400) As of August 24th, he was appointed to new position, military attaché to Japanese Legation in Helsinki. (JACAR, Ref.B14090846200) There used to be an army office in Helsinki before the outbreak of the Winter War (1939-1940), a war between Finland and the Soviet Union. But, ever since, Colonel Toshio Nishimura, military attaché to Finland and Sweden (1938-1940), had moved to Stockholm. Thus, Onouchi probably tried to contact Tokyo through Nishimura for further instructions.

It is said that he took some of his former informants (including Rybikowski) and ex-Riga army office staffs with him on the journey to Sweden. Anyway, the only confirmed fact regarding the trip was that on October 24th, Swedish Embassy in Helsinki sent a telegraph to Stockholm requesting the permission for Onouchi 'alone' to enter Sweden on October 30th.

Figure 26. Legation of Japan in Finland. Address: 11B. Puistokatu (Parkgatan) , Helsinki.Japanese Army office in Helsinki was located inside the Legation until 1944 when the building was heavily damaged by the Soviet bombing and the Army office moved to Kauniainen (Grankura). Courtesy: Finnish Defence Force Archive (*SA-Kuva*)

Appendix

Military Attaches to Japanese Legation in Latvia (1928-1940)

Names (SURNAME)		Position	Terms in Office
Shigeyasu SUZUKI*		Colonel (Army)	Aug.1928-Jun.1930
Hikosaburo HATA*		Major (Army)	Jun.1930-Jun.1931
Osato KAWAMATA		Captain (Army)	Jul.1931-Jul.1933
Tsutomu OUCHI		Lieutenant Colonel (Army)	Aug.1933-Dec.1935
Makoto ONODERA		Major (Army)	Jan.1936-Apr.1938
Tamotsu TAKATSUKI		Major (Army)	May.1938-May.1939
Hiroshi ONOUCHI		Lieutenant Colonel (Army)	Jun.1939-Sep.1940

*Joint administrations by military attaches to Poland (non-residence in Latvia)

Mitsunobu SUZUKI*		Lieutenant Colonel (Navy)	Sep.1939-Jan.1940

*Temporary assignment from Japanese Navy office in Berlin, shortly before his formal assignment as a military attaché to Romania.

Riga Army Office Staffs

Nina Shvangiradze		Secretary (Georgian Latvian)	1936-1940
Maria Maglakelidze		Secretary (Georgian Latvian)	1936-1940
Zelma		Housekeeper (Latvian)	
Luize Kindelo		Cook (Estonian)	1937-1940
Marie		Nurse (Estonian)	

Assistant Military Attaché (Resided in Estonia, 1938)

Takeharu SHIMANUKI		Captain (Army)	Feb.1938-Sep.1938

Army Researchers in Riga Residence (1923-1929?)

Noritsune SHIMIZU		Captain (Army)	Mar. 1924-Apr.1926
Torashiro KAWABE		Captain (Army)	Mar. 1926-Aug. 1928
Genzo YANAGIDA		Captain (Army)	1927-1929?

Military Officers on Special Missions (1919-1925)

Michitaro KOMATSUBARA		Captain (Army)	1919-1922 (Estonia)
Kenichi IKENAKA		Lieutenant Colonel (Navy)	1924-1925 (Latvia)

Bibliography

Bowyer, R. (2007). *Dictionary of Military Terms* (3rd ed.).
London, United Kingdom: A&C Black Publishers Ltd.

"Changes of Japanese Military Attaché". *Latvijas Kareivis*, July 21st 1931, p.1.

"Estonia and Japan". *Tokyo Asahi Shimbun,* July 21st 1919, p.3.

"Group of Japanese Military Officers visited Kiviõli". *Uus Eesti,* June 4th 1939, p.3.

Ilmjärv, M. (2003). The Baltic States Military and Their Foreign and Defence Policies 1933-38. *Acta Historica Tallinnensia, 7,* Page 89.

JACAR(Japan Centre for Asian Historical Records). "Regarding the Trips of the Researcher on the Soviet Affairs inside Russia". Ref. C01006107900, Dai Nikki, Otsushu, 1928. (NIDS)

JACAR (Japan Centre for Asian Historical Records) "The Order of Preparing Weapons for the Donation to Estonia, from Firearms Division, the Ministry of Army to the Commander of Tokyo Arsenal". Ref.C01004065200, Mitsu Dainikki, Vol. 2, 1935. (NIDS)

JACAR (Japan Centre for Asian Historical Records) "Exchanging Small Arms and Pistols with Nation of Estonia". Ref. C01006736600, Dainikki, Otsushu, 1935. (NIDS)

JACAR (Japan Centre for Asian Historical Records). "Procuring Ordnance". Ref.C01006653500, Dainikki, Otsushu, 1935. (NIDS)

JACAR(Japan Center for Asian Historical Records). Ref.C01003722800、Mitsu Dainikki, 2 of 6, 1927(NIDS)

JACAR(Japan Centre for Asian Historical Records). "Sending Army Officers to Overseas ". Ref. C01006039400, Dai Nikki, Otsushu, 1927. (NIDS)

JACAR (Japan Centre for Asian Historical Records) "Regarding the Shipment of Ammunition". Ref. C01004067100, Mitsu Dainikki, Vol. 2, 1935. (NIDS)

JACAR (Japan Centre for Asian Historical Records) "Regarding the Donation of Handgun Live Bullets to Estonia". Ref. C01006855500, Dainikki, Otsushu, 1936. (NIDS)

JACAR (Japan Centre for Asian Historical Records) "Regarding the Information of the Great Purge in the Soviet Union". Ref.C01004397400.
Mitsu Dainikki, Volume 12, 1937. (NIDS)

JACAR (Japan Centre for Asian Historical Records) "Assigning Officer in Foreign Country as Assistant Officer at Local Site". Ref. C01004434500, Mitsu Dainikki, Vol. 4, 1938. (NIDS)

JACAR (Japan Centre for Asian Historical Records) "Expatriation of Army Officer". Ref. C01004299100, Mitsu Dainikki, Vol. 5, 1937. (NIDS)

JACAR (Japan Centre for Asian Historical Records) "Regarding the Return of the Assistant Officer". Ref.C01004593400, Mitsu Dainikki, Vol. 4, 1939. (NIDS)

JACAR (Japan Center for Asian Historical Records). Ref.C01001775900.
The request of sending a letter of attorney rearding the registration of the transfer of the Berlin army office. Dainikki Kou. 1939. (NIDS)

JACAR (Japan Centre for Asian Historical Records). "The Tallinn Diplomat Office". Gaimusho Kiroku, Zaigai Teikoku Koukan Kankei Zakken.
Ref.B14090246400. 1939. (MoFA Diplomatic Archives)

JACAR (Japan Centre for Asian Historical Records). "MoFA Staff Movements".Gaimusho Ho Volume 24. Ref.B13091825000. (MoFA Diplomatic Archives)

JACAR (Japan Centre for Asian Historical Records). "Tallinn Diplomat Office". Zaigai Teikoku-Koukan Kankei Zakken (Zaiman, Zaishi Koukan Nozoku) (Kyu Kazokukaikan Roumon Zaibei taishikan he ichiku ni kansuru ken wo fukumu). (M-1-3-0-1_6). Ref.B14090274900. 1940. (MoFA Diplomatic Archives)

JACAR (Japan Centre for Asian Historical Records) "Documents regarding the Diplomatic Missions in the Baltic States" (M-2-1-0-60) Ref.B14091188400. 1940. (MoFA Diplomatic Archives)

JACAR (Japan Centre for Asian Historical Records). Zaigai Koukan Tsuki Bukan Ninmen Kankei Zatsubo Volume 5. (M-2-1-0-12_005). Ref.B14090846200. (MoFA Diplomatic Archives)

JACAR (Japan Centre for Asian Historical Records). Ref.B03040748900. Miscellaneas related to propaganda / Advisers and public relations men financed by the government and other publicity expenditures / Foreigners Section Volume 9.(1-3-1-35_1_2_009)(MoFA Diplomatic Archives)

JACAR (Japan Centre for Asian Historical Records). Ref.B15100944400. Miscellaneas related to the diplomatic missions in the Western countries.(6-1-2-76_2) (MoFA Diplomatic Archives)

JACAR (Japan Centre for Asian Historical Records). Riga Diplomat Office. Ref.B15100944400、ZaigaiTeikoku Koukan Zakken/Zai Oubei Kakkan (6-1-2-76_2). (MoFA Diplomatic Archives)

JACAR(Japan Centre for Asian Historical Records). Ref. B14090839400. Zaigai Koukan Tsuki Bukan Ninmen Kankei Zassan Volume 3 (M-2-1-0-12_003). (MoFA Diplomatic Archives)

JACAR (Japan Centre for Asian Historical Records) Gaimusho-Ho. Volume 17. (Gai/Hou 17). Ref.B13091661400. (MoFA Diplomatic Archives)

JACAR (Japan Centre for Asian Historical Records). Ref.B03040748900. Volume 9. (Senden Kankei Zakken/Shokutaku Hojyokinsikyuu sendensha sonota sendenhi sishutsu kankei/gaikokujin-no-bu/dai-kyu-kan) (1-3-1-35_1_2_009). (MoFA Diplomatic Archives)

Japan – Brave Nation in the Far East". *Sakala*, January 14th 1935, p. 2.

"Japanese Military Attaché Major Kawamata". *Latvijas Kareivis*, September 23rd 1932, p.1.

"Japanese Legation in Tallinn Residence". *Uus Eesti*, December 30th 1939, p.3.

"Japanese Officer left Estonia". *Sakala*, March 10th 1934, p.2.

"Japanese Officer left Estonia". *Lääne Teataja*, March 10th 1934, p.3.

"Japan made a Provisional Recognition of Estonia". *Tokyo Asahi Shimbun*, March 23rd 1919, p.2.

"Japanese Presented the Credentials". *Latvijas Kareivis*, October 30th 1928, Page 1.

"Japanese Military Attaché in Narva-Jõesuu". *Uus Eesti*, July 15th 1939, Page 6.

"Japanese Diplomats in Narva-Jõesuu". *Uus Eesti*, July 4th 1939, Page 5.

"Japanese Military Attaché left Estonia". *Uus Eesti*, May 10th 1939, Page 5.

"Japanese Representative in Pärnu". Uus Eesti Pärnu Uudised, July 15th 1938,

Page 1.

Juurvee, Ivo. (2013). *Protection of State Secrets in the Republic of Estonia. (Riigisaladuse kaitse Eesti Vabariigis 1918–1940).* Tartu, Estonia: Tartu Ülikooli Kirjastus.

Juurvee, Ivo. (2003). The Structure of Estonian and Latvian Military Intelligence Services in 1930s: Some Comparisons with the German Abwehr. (*Eesti ja Läti sõjaväeluure struktuur 1930-ndail: võrdlus Saksa Abwehriga*). *Annual Publication of Estonian War Museum 2003.*

Kawabe, T. (1962). *From Ichigaya-Dai to Ichigaya-Dai: The Memoir of the Last Vice Chief of the General Staff.* Tokyo, Japan: Jiji Press Co., Ltd.

Kuromiya, H., & Mamoulia, G. (2016). *The Eurasian Triangle: Russia, The Caucasus and Japan, 1904-1945*. Berlin, Germany: Walter de Gruyter GmbH.

Kuromiya, H. (2011) . The Mystery of Nomonhan, 1939.
The Journal of Slavic Military Studies, 24(4), p.659-677.

Laidoner, J. (1953). *Johan Laidoner.*
Örebro, Sweden: Tryckcentralen.

Levent, S. (2012). The Eurasian Policy of Imperial Japan and The Axis Allies: A Focus on Islamic Populations and Anti-Soviet Policies (*Senkan-Ki ni okeru Nihon no 'Yurashia Seisaku' to Sangoku Doumei*), *Asia Kenkyu, 58(1),* p.69-88.

Okabe, N. (2014). *Onodera Makoto: God of Espionage.* (*Chouhou no Kamisama to yobareta Otoko: Rengoukoku ga osoreta Jyoho-Shikan Onodera Makoto no Ryugi*). Tokyo, Japan: PHP Institute.

Okabe, N. (2012). *Disappeared Yalta Report: The Struggle of Intelligence Officer Makoto Onodera. (Kieta Yaruta Mitsuyaku Kinkyuden: Jyoho-Shikan Onodera*

Makoto no Kodoku na Tatakai). Tokyo, Japan: Shinchosha.

Onodera, Y. (2007). *Makoto Onodera: General who did not want war. (Estonian publication of Baruto-kai no Hotori nite, 1985).* Tallinn, Estonia: Eesti Entsüklopeediakirjastus.

Onodera, Y. (2016). *People in Shores of the Baltic Sea.* (*Baruto-kai no Hotori no Hitobito*). Tokyo, Japan: Shinpyouron Co., Ltd.

Onodera, M. (1992). *The Record of Intelligence Activities of Major General Makoto Onodera 1935-1946: Volume 1.* (*Rikugun Shoshou Onodera Makoto Jyoho Kinmu Kiroku 1935-1946: Jyo-kan*). Yasukuni Archives, Tokyo. Reference Number: 79448.

Päewaleht. (1921, June 1). New Japanese Diplomatic Representative to Estonia. p.4.

"Profiles of the Three Generals". *Tokyo Asahi Shimbun*, April 9th 1943, Page 1.

"Representative of Japanese Military in Pärnu". *Postimees*, July 16th 1938, Page 4.

"Recognition of Latvia". *Tokyo Asahi Shimbun.* March 13th 1920, p.3.

"Recognition of Lithuania". *Tokyo Asahi Shimbun.* December 24th 1922, p.1

Saarsen, V. (1978). *What I saw. (See mis ma nägin).*
Stockholm, Sweden: Riksby-Tryck.

Shimanuki, T. (1988). *Memorial Writing for Tadamasa Shimanuki. (Tsuto-Bunshu Shimanuki Tadamasa).* Saitama, Japan: Taikosha.

"Soviet No Menace to a Strong Japan, says Riga Attache". *The Japan Times*, May

30th 1938, p.1.

Strategic Services Unit (SSU), the U.S. War Department. (September 30, 1946). *Japanese Wartime Intelligence Activities in Northern Europe.* Reference Number: DB#1225.

Strategic Services Unit (SSU), the U.S. War Department. (September 30, 1946). *Japanese Wartime Military Missions in Europe.*
Reference Number: DB#1245.

Strategic Services Unit (SSU), the U.S. War Department. (September 25, 1946). *ONODERA, Major General Makoto -- Biographical Sketch of.*
Reference Number: DB#1226.

"Soviet Merchant Ship Sunken in Estonia." *Yomiuri Shimbun*, September 29th 1939, Page 1.

Tamman, T. (2014). *Portrait of a Secret Agent.*
York, United Kingdom: Thousand Eyes Publishing.

"Terrorism in Beijing". Tokyo Asahi Shimbun, December 1st 1940, Page 1.

"The Results of the General Elections in the Baltic States". *Tokyo Asahi Shimbun*, July 19th 1940, Page 3.

"The Legation in Latvia established". *Tokyo Asahi Shimbun*, September 4th 1929, Page 3.

"The Army Commander receives". *Rigasche Rundschau*, September 17th 1938, Page 7.

"Tragedy of Minor Powers". *Tokyo Asahi Shimbun*, July 28th 1940, Page 5.

Kasekamp, A. (2010). *A History of the Baltic States.*
London, United Kingdom: Palgrave Macmillan.

Kuromiya, H., & Mamoulia, G. (2016). *The Eurasian Triangle: Russia, The Caucasus and Japan, 1904-1945*. Walter de Gruyter GmbH.
https://www.degruyter.com/view/product/469152?format=EBOK

Kuromiya, H. (2011). The Mystery of Nomonhan, 1939.
The Journal of Slavic Military Studies, 24(4), p.659-677.

"Mentality of Japanese (Jaapani Vaim)". *Sõdur*. (1934, March 3). p.248-250.

"MoFA to establish Legation in Latvia". *Tokyo Asahi Shimbun*, July 5th 1928, Page 1.

Ministry of Foreign Affairs of Japan (MoFA). (2011). *Documents on Japanese Foreign Policy (Nihon Gaikou Bunsho) Volume 3.* Tokyo, Japan: Rokuichi-Shobo.

Ministry of Foreign Affairs of Japan (MoFA). (2011). *Documents on Japanese Foreign Policy (Nihon Gaikou Bunsho) Volume 2.* Tokyo, Japan: Rokuichi-Shobo.

Nishiura, S. (2014). *The Secret Records of the Showa Army. (Showa Rikugun Hiroku).* Tokyo, Japan: Nikkei Publishing Inc.

Von Rauch, O. (1974). *The Baltic States: The Years of Independence 1917-1940.*
C. Hurst & Company Ltd.

Yamazaki, M. (2010). Lightening War in Poland (*Poland Dengekisen*).
Tokyo, Japan: Gakken Publishing Co., Ltd.

www.ingramcontent.com/pod-product-compliance
Ingram Content Group UK Ltd.
Pitfield, Milton Keynes, MK11 3LW, UK
UKHW050613260726
13967UKWH00008B/2845